B C D E

H I J K

O P Q R

W X Y Z

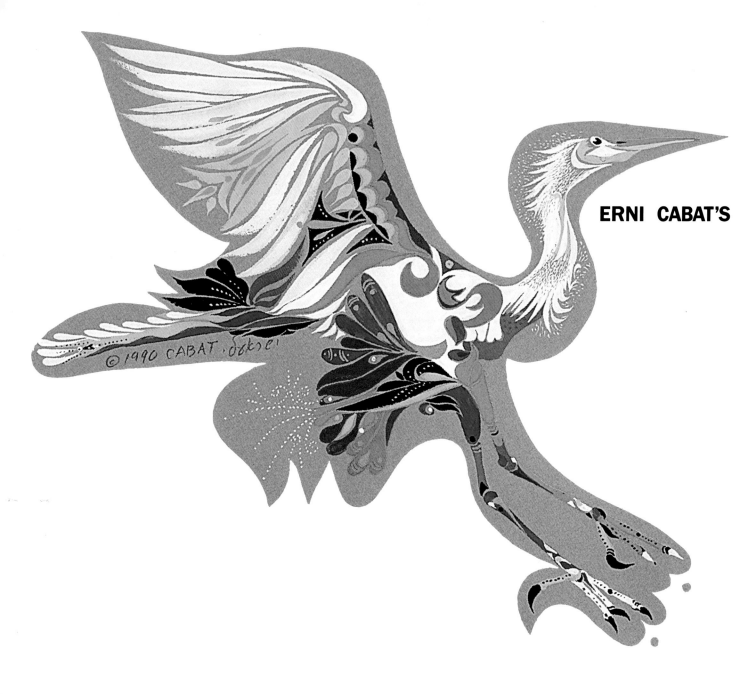

**ERNI CABAT'S**

© 1990 CABAT

MAGICAL

# ABC

ANIMALS AROUND THE FARM

© 1990 . CABAT . 66/001

HARBINGER HOUSE

HARBINGER HOUSE, INC.
Tucson, Arizona

Illustrations copyright © 1992 by Erni Cabat
Text copyright © 1992 by Michael J. Rule

Printed in Mexico

*Designed by Erni Cabat*

Library of Congress Cataloging-in-Publication Data

Cabat, Erni.
     [Magical ABCs]
     Erni Cabat's magical ABCs : animals around the farm / paintings by
Erni Cabat ; verse and notes by Michael J. Rule.
         p.   cm.
     Summary: Portrays domestic animals from A to Z, with a glossary of
basic facts and curiosities about all the animals represented.
ISBN 0-943173-73-6
     1. Cabat, Erni—Juvenile literature. 2. Animals in art—Juvenile
literature.   [1. Domestic animals. 2. Alphabet.]   I. Rule,
Michael J., 1949–   .   II. Title.   III. Title: Magical ABCs.
ND237.C14A4   1992
759.13—dc20
[E]                                                        90-5242

86578

# LETTERS!

## ARE MAGIC!

## LETTERS ARE FUN!

Put them together and see how they run!
Mix 'em and match 'em and pile 'em sky-high—
Use them for questions like WHO ?
                                    WHAT ?
                          and WHY ?

Twenty-six letters are all that we've got.
When you think of it, that's not a whole lot.
But imagine everything those letters can be—
As small as an ant, as BIG as a tree!

With letters there isn't a thing you can't name,
Which turns out to be a pretty good game.
From A to Z, just shake a few loose
To spell funny names like *egret* and *goose!*

You can name all the animals that live 'round the farm,
Out in the field, or in the big barn.
Some are wild and hide when you come;
The tame ones *like* people and come on the run.

But friendly or shy, wild or tame,
These animals all have one thing the same.
To find them you'd go to the farm to look—
They're not *wild* wild.  *That's another book!*

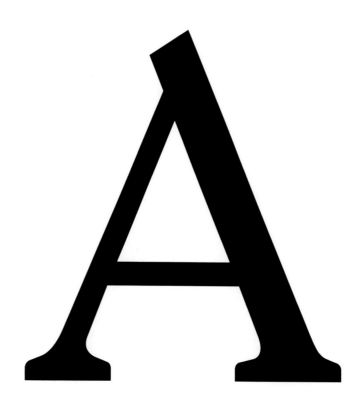

APPALOOSA

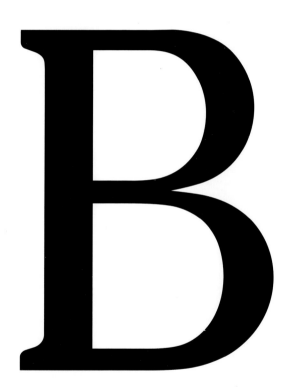

BUTTERFLY

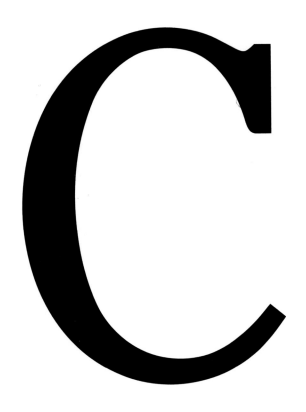

COW

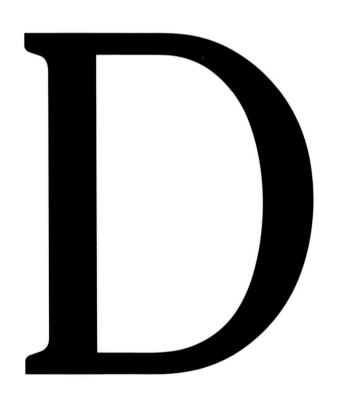

DOG

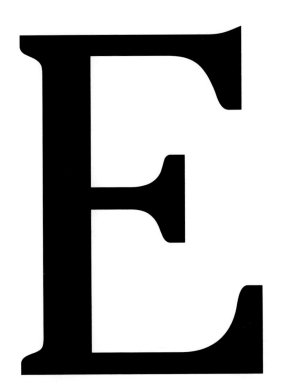

EGRET

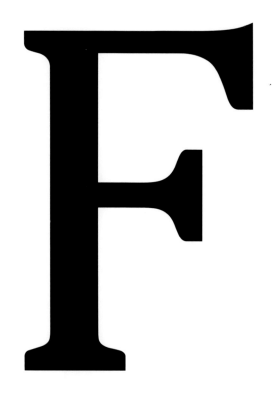

FROG

GOOSE

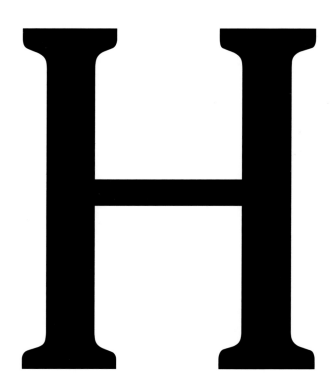

HONEYBEE

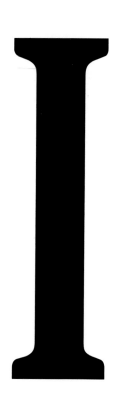

INCHWORM

CABAT. ©1990

JACKRABBIT

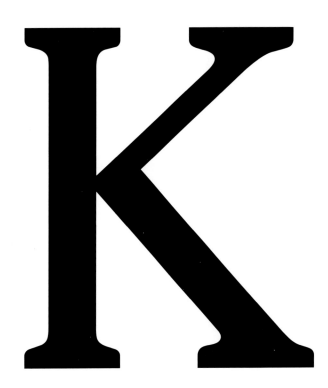

KATYDID

© 1990 · CABAT ·

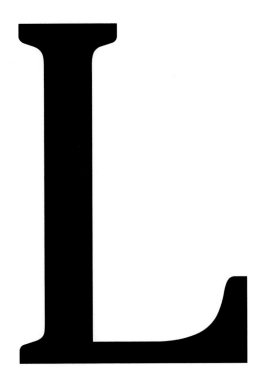

LARK

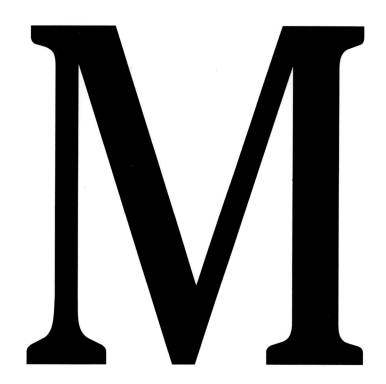

MOUSE

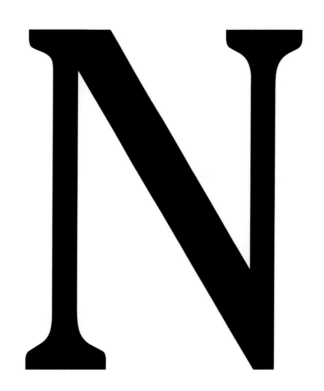

NANNY GOAT

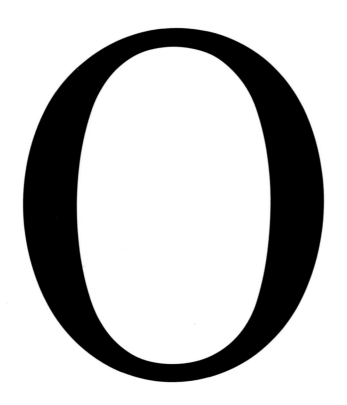

OWL

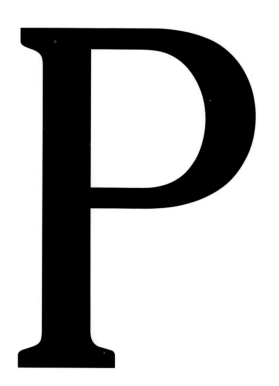

PIG

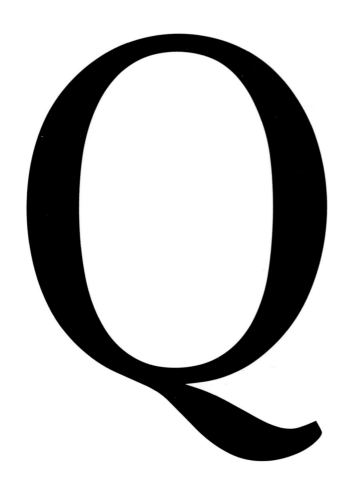

QUAIL

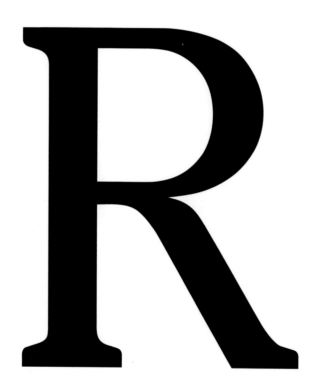

ROOSTER

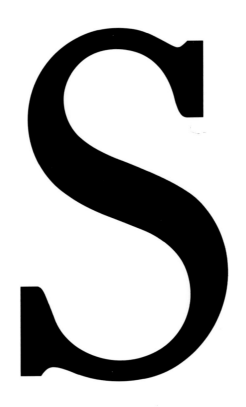

SHEEP

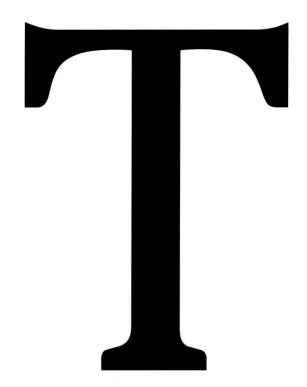

TURKEY

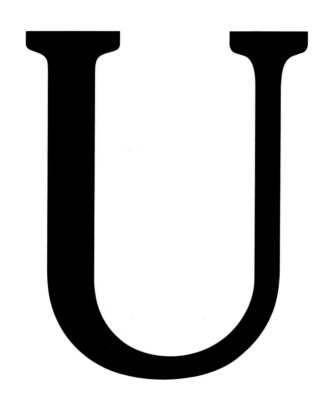

UPSIDE–DOWN CAT

VOLE

WEASEL

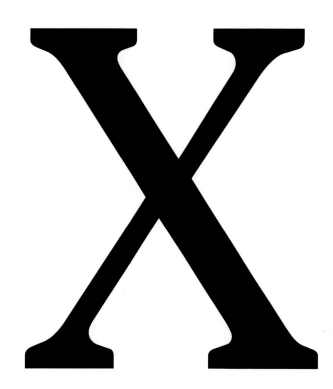

FOX

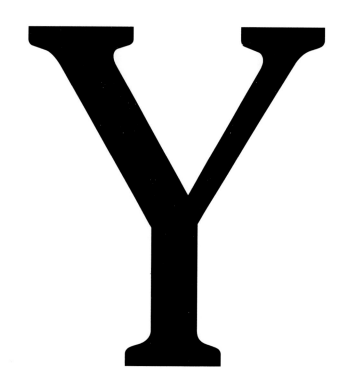

YELLOWTHROAT

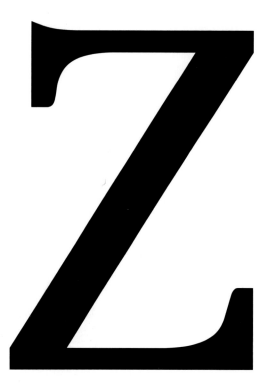

LIZARD

# ABOUT THE ANIMALS

**A**PPALOOSA . . . The Appaloosa horse is named after the Palousa River in Idaho. The Nez Perce who lived there raised strong, fast horses with spotted rumps and striped hooves.

Spotted horses just like the Appaloosa have been around a long time. Two hundred centuries ago, people painted pictures of them on the walls of caves in Europe. The ancient Egyptians used spotted horses, and so did the ancient Chinese. Buffalo Bill Cody rode Appaloosas in his Wild West Show. Cowboys like to ride Appaloosas because they're smart and brave and can turn very sharp corners, which helps the cowboys catch cows.

**B**UTTERFLY . . . There are about 20,000 different kinds of butterflies, and they live almost everywhere in the world. The biggest is the size of a dinner plate; the smallest would barely cover the tip of your little finger.

Butterflies come in every color you can think of. Their wings are covered with tiny scales, like the scales of a fish, only much smaller.

**C**OW . . . Cows have been farm animals for thousands of years. In 1493, when Columbus made his second voyage to the New World, he brought cows with him.

The average dairy cow gives more than four gallons of milk every day. But she can't give any milk at all unless she's had a baby — called a *calf.* Then she can give milk for almost a year.

**D**OG . . . There are hundreds of breeds of dogs. The Chihuahua is the smallest, even smaller than a cat. The tallest is the Irish wolfhound, which stands three feet high at the shoulder. The Saint Bernard is the heaviest breed; it weighs as much as 200 pounds, which is pretty heavy even for a person.

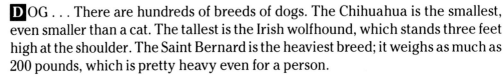

Dogs hear and smell much better than people do, but they don't see as well. In fact, dogs are color blind — to a dog, everything looks like the picture on a black-and-white TV.

**E**GRET . . . Egrets live in every part of the world except the South Pole. They wade through the water on their long, skinny legs and catch fish and frogs and other creatures with their long, skinny beaks. And when an egret flies, it folds up its long, skinny neck like the letter S.

A hundred years ago, egrets almost became extinct because people liked to use their feathers to decorate ladies' hats. So now it's against the law to hurt an egret.

**F**ROG . . . There are 3,000 different kinds of frogs. Some are the size of a pencil eraser; some are bigger than a lunch box. Some live in water, some live on the land, and some burrow down into the dirt. Some even live in trees. One kind of tree frog can sail through the air, using the webbing between its toes like a parachute!

Frogs are very valuable animals. A frog's tongue is like a sticky rubber band, which it uses to catch lots and lots of insects. And many other animals — such as egrets — eat frogs for food.

**G**OOSE . . . Geese are bigger than ducks and smaller than swans. Every spring and fall, they *migrate* — large flocks of them travel many miles between their winter and summer homes. But they're so heavy they have to run a few steps before they can even take off.

The mother goose and the father goose stay together for life. The baby goose, called a *gosling,* takes more than a day to hatch from its egg. Together with the rest of the flock, they migrate to the same places year after year. Sometimes you can see them flying across the sky in a big V, which makes it easier for everybody to see where they're going. It makes flying easier, too.

**H**ONEYBEE . . . The honeybee is the only insect that makes food that humans eat. Honey is *supposed* to be for the bees to eat during the winter, but they make enough for people to eat, too.

Every hive has three kinds of bees — one queen and many workers and drones. The queen lays eggs, with the help of the drones. The workers gather pollen from flowers and take care of the hive and protect it. When a worker bee finds a good spot to gather pollen, which the bees use for food, it does a special dance to tell the other bees how to find the place!

**I**NCHWORM . . . Farmers don't like the inchworm *at all.* Every day an inchworm eats its weight in leaves. That causes a lot of damage around the farm. Like acrobats, the worms drop on strands of fine silk from leaf to leaf, eating their way from tree to tree.

Inchworms are the caterpillars of some kinds of moths. They don't have legs under the middle part of their bodies, so they can't walk all at once, like most caterpillars do. Instead, they move the front half and then the back half hurries to catch up.

**J**ACKRABBIT . . . Jackrabbits are very different from rabbits, even though they look a lot alike. Newborn baby rabbits are helpless — they have no hair and their eyes are sealed shut. But jackrabbits, which are also called *hares,* are born with a full coat of fur and they can see right away. Rabbits are born in underground nests, while jackrabbits are born right out in the open.

Jackrabbits are a lot bigger, too. Some grow to over 30 inches long — which might be as big as *you!*

**K**ATYDID . . . The katydid is an insect that looks a little like a big grasshopper. But grasshoppers eat plants and cause lots of damage; most katydids eat other insects, which is much better for farmers and gardeners.

At night, the male katydid makes a loud noise by rubbing his wings together. The noise, which helps him meet female katydids, sounds like *Katy-did.* That's where that funny-sounding name comes from.

**L**ARK . . . Larks live in many areas of the world. They like to build their nests in fields and pastures and other places where there's lots of open land. Farmers love to hear the larks sing, because their beautiful song means winter is almost over. Farmers also like larks because they eat lots and lots of insects.

Larks migrate in huge flocks. Early in the spring, the male lark arrives and claims his territory. A little later, the female arrives and builds a nest, flat on the ground. Sometimes she'll put it right inside the hoofprint of a cow or a horse!

**M**OUSE . . . Mice are cute little animals, but farmers don't like them because they cause a lot of damage around the farm. Mice are *always* hungry, and they like to burrow into things with their sharp front teeth, which are shaped especially for gnawing.

There are many different kinds of mice. Some have big toes that work like human thumbs, which makes it easy for them to grab things. One kind of mouse is so tiny it climbs up a stalk of grass to build its nest!

**N**ANNY GOAT . . . People have been raising goats for a long, long time. Goats and cows give people the same things, such as milk. But goats can live on cold mountains and in hot deserts, places where cows would be *very* unhappy.

A female goat is called a *nanny* goat. Her milk is very much like cow's milk, but it's sweeter, richer, and easier for people to digest. People can use it to make cheese and yogurt, too. Even ice cream!

**O**WL . . . Owls hunt at night. They have special feathers on their wings that let them fly without making any sound at all. That makes it easier for them to go hunting, because the mice, gophers, and other creatures they eat have pretty good hearing!

Owls also have very good eyesight, and they hear wonderfully well. An owl's ears are not both the same — each is shaped a little differently, and each hears a little differently. That helps the owl know exactly where a sound came from and from how far away — which is good to know when you're trying to find your dinner in the middle of the night!

**P**IG . . . People say such bad things about pigs! But pigs are very smart. Some people even keep pigs for pets, right in the house! Pigs keep themselves cleaner than most animals on the farm, too; they like to wallow in mud only because it helps them stay cool.

Some pigs weigh as much as 500 pounds when they grow up. That's as much as three or four grown-ups! Mother pigs, called *sows,* have lots of babies at one time — sometimes more babies than you have fingers and toes. Imagine that!

**Q**UAIL . . . The quail is about the size of a pigeon but has a shorter tail. And, like pigeons, quails come in all sorts of colors.

Quails live on the ground, hunting for seeds and insects to eat. They even make their nests on the ground, where they lay as many as 15 eggs at a time. With their short, rounded wings, quails can spring into the air and fly away very fast indeed when someone surprises them.

**R**OOSTER . . . People have raised chickens for thousands of years. Ancient peoples admired the male chicken, called a *rooster*, because he is brave and proud, and because he helps start the day by crowing *cock-a-doodle-doo* every morning as the sun comes up.

There are probably more chickens in the world than any other kind of bird. Farmers raise chickens for food, but did you know that many people raise chickens as a hobby, too? That's because there are so many interesting and beautiful kinds. In Japan, they raise a chicken with a tail that can grow to be 18 feet long. That's as long as a *big* car!

**S**HEEP . . . There are almost 1,000 different kinds of sheep—more than any other type of farm animal. Sheep are close relatives of goats; like goats and cows, sheep have a special stomach that lets them eat grass and hay.

Some kinds of sheep have big, curly horns; others don't have any horns at all. Sheep can live in dry desert areas and in rough mountains, where most farm animals can't.

**T**URKEY . . . All turkeys today come from wild turkeys that lived only in North America. Native Americans were the first to raise them. The early explorers took the big birds to Europe; people liked them so much that now farmers raise them all over the world!

The turkey's head and neck are covered with bumpy skin that changes color, from red to blue to white, depending on what mood the bird is in. Wouldn't it be funny if people did that?

**U**PSIDE-DOWN CAT . . . In Egypt, way back in the time of the pharaohs, people worshipped cats because they thought cats had magical powers.

There are special parts, like mirrors, inside cats' eyes to help them see in the dark. But when it's light outside, people see better than cats do. Cats have wonderful hearing; they can hear lots of sounds that humans can't. Maybe that's why they always look so smug—they know things we don't!

**V**OLE . . . The vole is a kind of field mouse. Voles eat seeds, bark, roots, and leaves. They have amazing appetites—every day, a vole will eat almost as much as it weighs. This tiny animal can actually kill a tree, by gnawing a ring all the way around its trunk.

A vole can have up to seven babies every three weeks, starting when it's only five weeks old! But many other animals eat voles, which is why you don't see them everywhere.

**W**EASEL . . . Farmers *like* weasels because they're such good hunters. Weasels help control the rodents—such as rats and voles—that damage the farmers' crops.

Some weasels change color with the seasons, turning white in winter and brown or gray in summer. With its long, skinny body and pointy head, a weasel can squeeze through any hole its head will fit through.

FO**X** . . . The fox is a close relative of the dog. Foxes live in many different parts of the world, from hot deserts in the south to windy snowfields in the north.

The female fox and the male fox usually stay together for life. Both parents help feed and take care of the babies, too. Most kinds of foxes have about four babies at a time. But the Arctic fox has as many as eleven!

**Y**ELLOWTHROAT . . . Yellowthroats are very common birds in many parts of the United States and Canada. They live in swamps and along streams and country roads where vines and bushes and weeds all grow together in big tangles.

Yellowthroats like to build their nests on the ground, or very close to it. They eat all sorts of insects, and when they sing, they sound like this: *witchity, witchity, witchity.* Or sometimes like this: *witch-a-wee-o, witch-a-wee-o.*

LI**Z**ARD . . . Some lizards move *very* slowly; others can run faster than a human. Some lay eggs; others give birth to live babies. Lizards come in lots of sizes, too, all the way from fingertip-size to the size of a small car!

Lizards have many tricks to help them escape from their enemies. Some can change colors. Some can glide on "wings" made of skin that stretches over special rib bones. And many can break off part of their tail when they want to. The tail twitches in such an interesting way the enemy stops to watch—while the lizard gets away.